Lerner SPORTS

SPORTS' GREATEST OF ALL TIME

PRO WRESTLING'S G.O.A.T.

HULK HOGAN, DWAYNE "THE ROCK" JOHNSON, AND MORE

JOE LEVIT

Lerner Publications ◆ Minneapolis

Lerner Sports is a database of high-interest biographies profiling notable sports superstars. Packed with fascinating facts, these bios explore the backgrounds, career-defining moments, and everyday lives of popular athletes. Lerner Sports is perfect for young readers developing research skills or looking for exciting sports content.

LERNER SPORTS FEATURES:

✔ Keyword search
✔ Topic navigation menus
✔ Fast facts
✔ Related bio suggestions to encourage more reading
✔ Admin view of reader statistics
✔ Fresh content updated regularly
and more!

Visit LernerSports.com **for a free trial!**

Lerner *SPORTS*

™

Lerner Publications Company
An imprint of Lerner Publishing Group, Inc.
241 First Avenue North
Minneapolis, MN 55401 USA

For reading levels and more information, look up this title at www.lernerbooks.com.

Main body text set in Aptifer Sans LT Pro.Typeface provided by Linotype AG.

Designer: Kim Morales

Library of Congress Cataloging-in-Publication Data

Names: Levit, Joseph, author.
Title: Pro wrestling's G.O.A.T. : Hulk Hogan, Dwayne "The Rock" Johnson, and more / Joe Levit.
Description: Minneapolis : Lerner Publications, [2022] | Series: Lerner sports. Greatest of all time (G.O.A.T.) | Includes bibliographical references and index. | Audience: Ages: 7–11 | Audience: Grades: 2–3 | Summary: "Who are the greatest pro wrestlers of all time? Readers will take a look at some of the best wrestlers of the past and present in this fun, fact-filled book"— Provided by publisher.
Identifiers: LCCN 2021000087 (print) | LCCN 2021000088 (ebook) | ISBN 9781728428611 (library binding) | ISBN 9781728431598 (paperback) | ISBN 9781728430812 (ebook)
Subjects: LCSH: Wrestlers—United States—Biography—Juvenile literature.
Classification: LCC GV1196.A1 L49 2022 (print) | LCC GV1196.A1 (ebook) | DDC 796.812092/2 [B]—dc23

LC record available at https://lccn.loc.gov/2021000087
LC ebook record available at https://lccn.loc.gov/2021000088

Manufactured in the United States of America
1-49398-49499-3/31/2021

TABLE OF CONTENTS

OFF THE TOP ROPE!

Pro wrestling is the ultimate performance art. It's been around since the late 1800s. Both men and women have a storied history of seeking the spotlight in a wrestling ring. But choosing the greatest of all time (G.O.A.T.) is difficult to do. That's because of the sports' wide range of styles, eras, and personalities.

FACTS AT A GLANCE

RIC FLAIR won eight National Wrestling Alliance (NWA) Championships and six World Championship Wrestling (WCW) Championships.

MANAMI TOYOTA has 13 five-star matches.

Many pro wrestlers have well-known finishing moves. **THE ROCK** had the People's Elbow, **RANDY SAVAGE** had the Flying Elbow Drop, and **STEVE AUSTIN** had the Stone Cold Stunner.

TRISH STRATUS won the WWE Women's Championship seven times. That's more than any woman in pro wrestling's history.

Countries showcase very different styles of wrestling. In Mexico, pro wrestling is called lucha libre. Mexican wrestlers, or luchadores, wear colorful masks and are high-flying artists. In puroresu, Japanese pro wrestling, wrestlers show off precise moves and technical skills. For American wrestlers, showmanship is as important as ability.

The largest pro wrestling league in the US is World Wrestling Entertainment (WWE). The league began in 1952. It was formerly known as the World Wide Wrestling Federation (WWWF) and World Wrestling Federation (WWF).

When pro wrestling started in the US, the wrestlers were mainly white. But equality in the sport improved over time. Bobo Brazil entered the ring in the 1950s. His matches against stars such as Buddy Rogers and Bruno Sammartino helped other Black Americans get into the sport.

It takes a lot to be a pro. The best wrestlers have several things in common. Wrestlers must sell rivalries by talking trash to their opponents. They need to have entrance music and a style that gets a crowd excited. They must be athletic and skilled in the ring. And they need a memorable finishing move.

Mexican wrestler Blue Demon

John Cena carries Triple H in their 2018 Greatest Royal Rumble match.

Top performers hold multiple wrestling titles. They've had five-star matches and are Hall of Fame material. You may not know all the names in this book. You may feel that someone important, such as John Cena, Lita, or The Undertaker, has been left out. To disagree with this list is okay. Debating who are the world's top pro wrestlers is what this book is all about.

#10

TRISH STRATUS

Trish Stratus's famous Stratusfaction move ended many matches. After putting an opponent in a headlock, she ran them toward the ropes. She kicked off the top rope and used that force to slam foes onto the mat and into submission.

For years Stratus had a feud with rival wrestler Lita. These two titans of women's wrestling had one of their best battles in 2004. Lita did a backflip off the top rope toward the end of the match, while Stratus was lying on the mat. Then Lita slammed into Stratus to complete the moonsault move. Lita won.

Stratus got her revenge two years later at the annual Unforgiven match. After a long contest, Stratus twisted up Lita's legs in a submission hold. Lita was forced to tap out. Stratus became the champion for a record seventh time.

TRISH STRATUS STATS

- She won seven WWE Women's Championships.

- She was named WWE Diva of the Decade in 2003.

- She is one of only four women to win a WWE Hardcore Championship.

- She was a four-time *Pro Wrestling Illustrated* Woman of the Year.

- She was inducted into the WWE Hall of Fame

#9

BRUNO SAMMARTINO

Bruno Sammartino was a top wrestler of the WWWF during the 1960s and 1970s. His strength and size alone made him a tough opponent every time he stepped into the ring. He famously used the bear hug finishing move to win many matches, helping him log the longest winning streak in wrestling history.

In 1963, Sammartino beat WWWF champion Buddy Rogers in 48 seconds to take the title. After that, Sammartino's winning streak lasted for a record 2,803 days. That's nearly eight years.

Sammartino often clashed with WWWF owner Vince McMahon Sr. McMahon supported wrestlers who put on a good show, even if they were involved in scandals. Sammartino wanted to focus on wrestling, *not* entertainment. He carried himself with class and dignity throughout his career. Sammartino's second winning streak lasted another 1,237 days.

BRUNO SAMMARTINO STATS

- He won two WWWF World Heavyweight Championships.

- He sold out Madison Square Garden in New York City a record 188 times.

- He lifted 565 pounds (256 kg) in 1959 to set an unofficial world record in the bench press.

- He was inducted into the Pro Wrestling Hall of Fame in 2002.

- He was inducted into the WWE Hall of Fame in 2013.

#8

SHAWN MICHAELS

Shawn Michaels's Sweet Chin Music kick, a move where he kicks his opponent's chin, is famous. The Heartbreak Kid played the part of both hated heel and fan favorite during his long career. He was a smaller but fierce competitor.

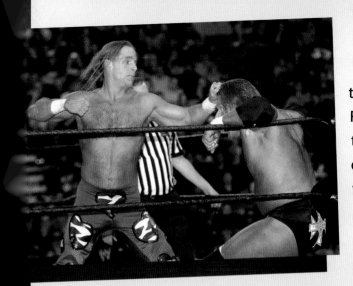

Michaels was the first to enter the ring in 1995's Royal Rumble. Despite that disadvantage, he outlasted the 29 other wrestlers to earn the victory. Michaels also had many classic fights with The Undertaker, including their famous cage match of 1997. It was a bloody battle. But Michaels, with help from wrestler Kane, pinned The Undertaker and won.

In the main event at WrestleMania 20, Michaels faced Triple H and Chris Benoit. Benoit won the heavyweight title, but Michaels's performance helped to make the match one fans will never forget.

SHAWN MICHAELS STATS

▷ He won one WWE Championship and three WWF Championships.

▷ He won three WWF Intercontinental Championships.

▷ He won the Royal Rumble in 1995 and 1996.

▷ He had two five-star matches.

▷ He was inducted into the Pro Wrestling Hall of Fame in 2017.

#7

"MACHO MAN" RANDY SAVAGE

"Macho Man" Randy Savage was famous for his intensity. His raspy voice gave every promo a threatening appeal. His outfits were torn, and the colors clashed. Wrestling fans everywhere recognized his oversized sunglasses.

Inside the ring, Savage took on every opponent with his high-energy style. He faced big stars and knocked them all down with his Flying Elbow Drop finishing move.

With his opponent on the ground, he would stand on the top rope. After getting the crowd pumped up, he would leap off the rope and drop on his opponent with his elbow.

Savage also had classic WrestleMania matches, including WrestleMania III. Before the match, Savage had damaged his opponent Ricky Steamboat's throat with a ring bell. Steamboat got his revenge at WrestleMania III and ended Savage's Intercontinental Champion streak. Savage lost, but he and Steamboat put on a great show in the ring that day.

"MACHO MAN" RANDY SAVAGE STATS

▷ He won **four WCW World Championships.**

▷ He won two WWF Championships.

▷ He won a WWF Intercontinental Championship.

▷ He had a small role as wrestler Bone Saw McGraw in the 2002 movie *Spider-Man.*

▷ He was inducted into the Pro Wrestling Hall of Fame in 2009.

DWAYNE "THE ROCK" JOHNSON

Wrestling is a way of life in the Johnson family. Johnson's father and grandfather were pro wrestlers. That's a lot to live up to. But Johnson made himself a household name and charmed audiences. His promos were some of the best in the business.

Johnson used a killer combination of moves to close out opponents. First, he would slam someone to the mat with the Rock Bottom. Then he'd drop the People's Elbow as a finishing move. Johnson had a lot of great victories. But many feel his best match was against Steve Austin in WrestleMania X-Seven. Austin hit Johnson with a chair at the end. He beat Johnson. But The Rock put up a hard fight.

These days Johnson is a movie star. He landed leading roles in action movies such as those in the *Fast & Furious* series. He also voiced the character Maui in *Moana*.

DWAYNE "THE ROCK" JOHNSON STATS

- He won **eight WWE** Championships.

- He won **five WWF Tag** Team Championships.

- He won **two WWF Intercontinental** Championships.

- He won **two WCW World Heavyweight** Championships.

- He won the **Royal Rumble in 2000**.

MANAMI TOYOTA

Japanese wrestler Manami Toyota began her career at 16. She had incredible athletic ability and passion and was a master of move combinations. Toyota would string together near-falls at a stunning speed. All of her performances showed strength and emotion.

Toyota faced off against Kyoko Inoue in 1992. They carried out a complex story line at a high pace. Many felt the two had the best skills in women's wresting. *Wrestling Observer Newsletter* journalist Dave Meltzer was one of them. He gave the match a five-star rating.

Toyota went against rival Toshiyo Yamada later that year in what became their famous Hair vs. Hair match. Whoever lost would have her hair cut in public. Toyota tossed Yamada with her fearless moves. Yamada flipped Toyota around with a series of suplexes. Toyota won, and she watched as Yamada's head was shaved in shame.

MANAMI TOYOTA STATS

► She won **two All Pacific Championships.**

► She won **four World Women's Wrestling Association (WWWA) World Single Championships.**

► She won **three WWWA World Tag Team Championships.**

► She twice won *Wrestling Observer Newsletter's* **Match of the Year.**

► She has **13 five-star matches.**

#4

BRET "THE HITMAN" HART

Bret Hart was a fantastic technical wrestler. He had the skill to make every match exciting, even when he faced inferior wrestlers in the ring. The Hitman paraded around in his famous pink outfits and sunglasses.

Hart came from a wrestling family. One of his best matches was against his younger brother Owen Hart at WrestleMania X. The two had been feuding for years. At the end of WrestleMania X, Owen Hart dragged his brother to the center of the mat. After wrapping his brother's legs around one of his own, the younger Hart flipped the older Hart onto his stomach. Owen Hart had used his brother's favored sharpshooter submission hold. The older Hart lost, but many fans feel it was the best WrestleMania match ever.

Another classic match saw Hart beat up Steve Austin, a heel. By the end of the WrestleMania 13 match the two had reversed roles. Hart became a heel, and Austin was the WWE's new baby face.

BRET "THE HITMAN" HART STATS

▷ He won **two WCW** Championships.

▷ He won **five WWF** Championships.

▷ He won the Royal Rumble in 1994.

▷ He had two five-star matches.

▷ He was inducted into the Pro Wrestling Hall of Fame in 2008.

HULK HOGAN

Hulk Hogan was not a great technical wrestler. But he was a superstar for two decades because he knew what people wanted to see. He could create convincing story lines in and outside the ring. This larger-than-life character had

Hogan competed against wrestling stars like Ric Flair, The Ultimate Warrior, and The Rock. But two WrestleMania matches are what he is best known for. He had to look up to his opponent in WrestleMania 3. André the Giant was more than 6 feet 8 (2 m) tall. Somehow Hogan picked up the Giant and slammed him to the mat to keep his title.

At WrestleMania 5, Hogan faced Randy Savage. Both men were in their primes. It was an active and entertaining match. But in the end Hogan beat Savage. He took the WWF Championship for himself.

HULK HOGAN STATS

- He won six WCW Championships.

- He won six WWF/WWE Championships.

- He won the Royal Rumble in 1990 and 1991.

- He played wrestler Thunderlips in the 1982 movie *Rocky III*.

- He was inducted into the Pro Wrestling Hall of Fame in 2003.

"STONE COLD" STEVE AUSTIN

Before "Stone Cold" Steve Austin entered the ring, fans heard breaking glass from the arena's loudspeakers. The sound meant Austin was on his way. Austin took the role of tough-looking fighter to new heights. He threw around threatening insults in promos. And the Texas Rattlesnake had a fantastic finishing move, the Stone Cold Stunner.

Austin began his career as a heel. But at WrestleMania 13, he took a turn for the good. He was in a submission match against Bret Hart. Austin was losing. Rather than submit, he passed out. His dedication made fans see him as a hero. It allowed him to become a baby face.

Four years later, Austin turned heel again. He was up against The Rock in WrestleMania X-Seven. No one could be disqualified in this match. So Austin beat up The Rock with a chair. He got the win but lost his good reputation.

"STONE COLD" STEVE AUSTIN STATS

- He won six WWF Championships.

- He won four WWF Tag Team Championships and two Intercontinental Championships.

- He won the Royal Rumble in 1997, 1998, and 2001.

- He had two five-star matches.

- He was inducted into the Pro Wrestling Hall

#1

RIC FLAIR

"The Nature Boy" Ric Flair had it all: looks, charm, wit, and style outside the ring, and strength and skill inside the ring. Flair's figure-four leglock is one of the best-known submission moves of all time. And he pumped up crowds with his promos.

He was the main attraction in the National Wrestling Alliance (NWA) and WCW wrestling leagues for a decade. Then he arrived in the WWE. He outlasted big names like The Undertaker and Hulk Hogan to win the 1992 Royal Rumble.

In 1989, Flair had his best fights in a set of three matches against Ricky Steamboat. Steamboat won the first match, and the second match was a draw. Flair took advantage of a Steamboat mistake in the third match. Flair got Steamboat in a classic cradle by wrapping one arm around Steamboat's neck and the other arm behind Steamboat's knee, and pinned Steamboat for the title.

RIC FLAIR STATS

> He won eight NWA Championships.

> He won six WCW Championships.

> He won the WWF Championship two times.

> He had 11 five-star matches.

> He was inducted into the Pro Wrestling Hall of Fame in 2006.

YOUR G.O.A.T.

IT'S YOUR TURN TO MAKE A LIST OF THE G.O.A.T. PRO WRESTLERS. Force your opponent into submission by doing some research. Carefully consider the rankings in this book. Then check out the Learn More section on page 31. There you'll see books and websites that will give you more information about the top pro wrestlers of the past and present. Talk to your librarian, who may have other resources to help you.

Once you're ready, make your list of the greatest pro wrestlers of all time. Then ask your friends to make their own lists and compare them. Do you have baby faces or heels that no one else listed? Are you missing someone that your friends think should be on your list? Talk it over, and try to convince them that your list is the G.O.A.T.!

WRESTLING FACTS

- Pro Wrestling journalist Dave Meltzer has ranked matches in the *Wrestling Observer Newsletter* since 1982.

- According to the Internet Wrestling Database, the longest wrestling match happened in 2015. Chris Hero (now known as Kassius Ohno) performed in a gauntlet match, a series of mini-matches, over three hours.

- A pro wrestler can win a match in multiple ways. Pin an opponent's shoulders to the mat for three seconds. Force an opponent to submit. Get an opponent disqualified by keeping the opponent outside the ring for too long. Or knock an opponent out.

- The first WrestleMania event was on March 31, 1985, at Madison Square Garden.

- *GLOW* was a TV series based on the 1980s Gorgeous Ladies of Wrestling group. Pro wrestler Kia Stevens, or Awesome Kong, acted on *GLOW*.

GLOSSARY

baby face: a "good-guy" wrestler meant to be cheered by fans

finishing move: an exciting, well-known way that a wrestler often uses to finish off an opponent

five-star match: a high match rating given by journalist Dave Metzler in the *Wrestling Observer Newsletter*. Metzler rates the matches based on their action and entertainment.

heel: a "villain" wrestler meant to be booed by fans

near-fall: when a wrestler almost pins an opponent but doesn't

promo: a short speech that wrestlers give to pump up the excitement for a match

Royal Rumble: when 30 wrestlers enter the ring one at a time to compete. The one who is still in the ring at the end is the winner.

submission hold: putting an opponent into a painful position so that the opponent will want to give up rather than go on

suplex: when a wrestler flips another wrestler over their own back to slam the opponent to the mat

tag team: when two wrestlers compete together against another pair for a title

tap out: when an opponent submits to another wrestler because a submission hold causes pain

WrestleMania: the WWE's annual top wrestling event

LEARN MORE

American Women's Wrestling
https://www.americanwomenswrestling.com/

Fishman, Jon M. *Boxing's G.O.A.T.: Muhammad Ali, Manny Pacquiao, and More.* Minneapolis: Lerner Publications, 2022.

Professional Wrestling Hall of Fame
https://www.pwhf.org

Shields, Brian, and Dean Miller. *35 Years of WrestleMania.* New York: DK, 2019.

Tracosas, L. J. *WWE Kicking Down Doors: Female Superstars Are Ruling the Ring and Changing the Game!* New York: DK, 2020.

World Wrestling Entertainment Network
https://www.wwe.com

INDEX

PHOTO ACKNOWLEDGMENTS

Image credits: AP Photo/Amr Nabil, p. 4; Luis Gutierrez/NortePhoto.com/Alamy Stock Photo, p. 6; AP Photo/Amr Nabil, p. 7; Don Arnold/WireImagey/Getty Images, pp. 8, 9 (top); Allstar Picture Library Ltd/Alamy Stock Photo, p. 9 (bottom); AP Photo/George Napolitano/MediaPunch/IPx, pp. 10, 11 (all); Z Sports Images/ Collection/Newscom, p. 12; Olivier Andrivon/Icon Sport//Getty Images, p. 13 (bottom); KMazur/WireImage/Getty Images, p. 13 (top); PF1/WENN/Newscom, p. 14; PHOTOlink/Alamy Stock Photo, pp. 15 (bottom), 20, 21 (top), 23 (bottom); John Barrett/PHOTOlink/Newscom, p. 15 (top); George Napolitano/FilmMagic/ Getty Images, p. 16; Kevin Mazur/WireImage/Getty Images, p. 17 (top); AP Photo/ Diego Corredor, p. 17 (bottom); Nippon News/Alamy Stock Photo, p. 18; Aflo Co. Ltd./Alamy Stock Photo, p. 19 (all); MediaPunch Inc/Alamy Stock Photo, p. 21 (bottom); AF archive/Alamy Stock Photo, p. 22; Yukio Hiraku/AFLO/Alamy Stock Photo, p. 23 (top); Globe Photos/ZUMAPRESS.com/Alamy Stock Photo, p. 24; AP Photo/Paul Abell, p. 25 (top); AP Photo/Jonathan Bachman, p. 25 (bottom); ZUMA Press, Inc./Alamy Stock Photo, p. 26; MediaPunch Inc/Alamy Stock Photo, p. 27 (top); Aflo Co. Ltd/Alamy Stock Photo, p. 27 (top); Kleka/Shutterstock.com, p. 28.

Cover: Chris Ryan - Corbis/Getty Images; MediaPunch Inc/Alamy Stock Photo; Inked Pixels/Shutterstock.com.